Plants
AND
Animals

AUTHORS

Mary Atwater
The University of Georgia

Prentice Baptiste
University of Georgia

Lucy Daniel
Rutherford County Schools

Jay Hackett
University of Northern Colorado

Richard Moyer
University of Michigan, Dearborn

Carol Takemoto
Los Angeles Unified School District

Nancy Wilson
Sacramento Unified School District

Lion

MACMILLAN / McGRAW-HILL

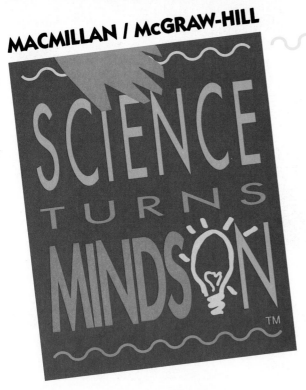

CONSULTANTS

Assessment:

Janice M. Camplin
Curriculum Coordinator, Elementary Science
Mentor, Western New York
Lake Shore Central Schools
Angola, NY

Mary Hamm
Associate Professor
Department of Elementary Education
San Francisco State University
San Francisco, CA

Cognitive Development:

Dr. Elisabeth Charron
Assistant Professor of Science Education
Montana State University
Bozeman, MT

Sue Teele
Director of Education Extension
University of California, Riverside
Riverside, CA

Cooperative Learning:

Harold Pratt
Executive Director of Curriculum
Jefferson County Public Schools
Golden, CO

Earth Science:

Thomas A. Davies
Research Scientist
The University of Texas
Austin, TX

David G. Futch
Associate Professor of Biology
San Diego State University
San Diego, CA

Dr. Shadia Rifai Habbal
Harvard-Smithsonian Center for Astrophysics
Cambridge, MA

Tom Murphree, Ph.D.
Global Systems Studies
Monterey, CA

Suzanne O'Connell
Assistant Professor
Wesleyan University
Middletown, CT

Environmental Education:

Cheryl Charles, Ph.D.
Executive Director
Project Wild
Boulder, CO

Gifted:

Sandra N. Kaplan
Associate Director, National/State Leadership
Training Institute on the Gifted/Talented
Ventura County Superintendent of Schools Office
Northridge, CA

Global Education:

M. Eugene Gilliom
Professor of Social Studies and Global Education
The Ohio State University
Columbus, OH

Merry M. Merryfield
Assistant Professor of Social Studies and Global
Education
The Ohio State University
Columbus, OH

Intermediate Specialist

Sharon L. Strating
Missouri State Teacher of the Year
Northwest Missouri State University
Marysville, MO

Life Science:

Carl D. Barrentine
Associate Professor of Biology
California State University
Bakersfield, CA

V.L. Holland
Professor and Chair, Biological Sciences
Department
California Polytechnic State University
San Luis Obispo, CA

Donald C. Lisowy
Education Specialist
New York, NY

Dan B. Walker
Associate Dean for Science Education and
Professor of Biology
San Jose State University
San Jose, CA

Literature:

Dr. Donna E. Norton
Texas A&M University
College Station, TX

Tina Thoburn, Ed.D.
President
Thoburn Educational Enterprises, Inc.
Ligonier, PA

Macmillan/McGraw-Hill School Division
10 Union Square East
New York, New York 10003

Printed in the United States of America

ISBN 0-02-274267-0 / 4

    6 7 8 9 VHJ 99 98 97 96 95 94

Giant toad

Mathematics:

Martin L. Johnson
Professor, Mathematics Education
University of Maryland at College Park
College Park, MD

Physical Science:

Max Diem, Ph.D.
Professor of Chemistry
City University of New York, Hunter College
New York, NY

Gretchen M. Gillis
Geologist
Maxus Exploration Company
Dallas, TX

Wendell H. Potter
Associate Professor of Physics
Department of Physics
University of California, Davis
Davis, CA

Claudia K. Viehland
Educational Consultant, Chemist
Sigma Chemical Company
St. Louis, MO

Reading:

Jean Wallace Gillet
Reading Teacher
Charlottesville Public Schools
Charlottesville, VA

Charles Temple, Ph. D.
Associate Professor of Education
Hobart and William Smith Colleges
Geneva, NY

Safety:

Janice Sutkus
Program Manager: Education
National Safety Council
Chicago, IL

Science Technology and Society (STS):

William C. Kyle, Jr.
Director, School Mathematics and Science Center
Purdue University
West Lafayette, IN

Social Studies:

Mary A. McFarland
Instructional Coordinator of
Social Studies, K-12, and
Director of Staff Development
Parkway School District
St. Louis, MO

Lily

Students Acquiring English:

Mrs. Bronwyn G. Frederick, M.A.
Bilingual Teacher
Pomona Unified School District
Pomona, CA

Misconceptions:

Dr. Charles W. Anderson
Michigan State University
East Lansing, MI

Dr. Edward L. Smith
Michigan State University
East Lansing, MI

Multicultural:

Bernard L. Charles
Senior Vice President
Quality Education for Minorities Network
Washington, DC

Cheryl Willis Hudson
Graphic Designer and Publishing Consultant
Part Owner and Publisher, Just Us Books, Inc.
Orange, NJ

Paul B. Janeczko
Poet
Hebron, MA

James R. Murphy
Math Teacher
La Guardia High School
New York, NY

Ramon L. Santiago
Professor of Education and Director of ESL
Lehman College, City University of New York
Bronx, NY

Clifford E. Trafzer
Professor and Chair, Ethnic Studies
University of California, Riverside
Riverside, CA

STUDENT ACTIVITY TESTERS

Jennifer Kildow
Brooke Straub
Cassie Zistl
Betsy McKeown
Seth McLaughlin
Max Berry
Wayne Henderson

FIELD TEST TEACHERS

Sharon Ervin
San Pablo Elementary School
Jacksonville, FL

Michelle Gallaway
Indianapolis Public School #44
Indianapolis, IN

Kathryn Gallman
#7 School
Rochester, NY

Karla McBride
#44 School
Rochester, NY

Diane Pease
Leopold Elementary
Madison, WI

Kathy Perez
Martin Luther King Elementary
Jacksonville, FL

Ralph Stamler
Thoreau School
Madison, WI

Joanne Stern
Hilltop Elementary School
Glen Burnie, MD

Janet Young
Indianapolis Public School #90
Indianapolis, IN

CONTRIBUTING WRITER

Don Schaub

3

Plants and Animals

Activities!

EXPLORE

TRY THIS

Features

Links

Music/Art Link

Literature Links

Social Studies Links

CAREERS

GLOBAL VIEW

SCIENCE TECHNOLOGY and Society

Focus on Technology

Focus on Environment

Departments

Plants and Animals

Foraminifera, a tiny protozoan

African elephants

Elephants are the largest land animals on Earth today. They grow from 3 to 3.5 meters tall (about 10 to 11 feet) and weigh up to 6 metric tons (about 7 tons). Blue whales are even bigger. They may grow 30 meters long (about 100 feet) and weigh 135 metric tons (about 150 tons). The heaviest flower we know about is the rafflesia, which grows in the tropical forests of southeast Asia. It weighs as much as 9 kilograms (about 20 pounds), measures from 0.9 to 1.2 meters in diameter (about 3 to 4 feet), and it smells bad!

You can't see the smallest living things without a microscope. They have only one cell. Scientists have probably not yet discovered many of the living things that share Earth with us. Living things come in many shapes and sizes, but they have some basic things in common.

All living things are made of cells. By the time you are fully grown, your body will contain about 100 trillion (100,000,000,000,000) cells! Think how many cells an elephant must have. But one-celled organisms are made of cells, too.

The first traces of life on Earth date back over 3 billion years. Every living thing since that time has carried on certain life functions such as growth and reproduction. Over a long period of time, life evolved from its earliest signs to its present forms.

It is the diversity of the life-forms that have evolved over time that you will be exploring in this unit. To understand similarities and differences, and to explain how living things have changed over time, scientists have organized and classified living things into different groups. This requires careful observation of the similarities and differences among living things.

Activity!

Life Around You

What You Need
Activity Log page 1

Look around you. In your *Activity Log*, list at least ten living things you see or you can think of. Like a scientist, think carefully about the similarities and differences among these living things. In your *Activity Log,* organize or classify your living things based on your observations. Now name the groups of living things you classified. Discuss your list with your classmates.

In the Try This Activity, you made up your own system of classification. How did you go about placing living things in groups? Did you have plants and animals? Did you have any other groups? Did you look at how they are made? Do they all have the same parts?

A system of classifying living things that people have been using for many years identifies five different groups or kingdoms. More groups may be added as people become aware of further differences among living things. In this unit you are going to explore only two of the kingdoms: plants and animals.

Minds On! In your *Activity Log* on page 2, write down as many reasons as you can for classifying plants and animals. Look back at your list from the Try This Activity. Did you classify living things in that activity for the same reasons that you did in this one? Why or why not? Did you classify plants and animals that are used as food? We don't just need plants and animals for food. How else do you interact with them? What would your life be like without them? ●

Why would you want to understand more about plants and animals?

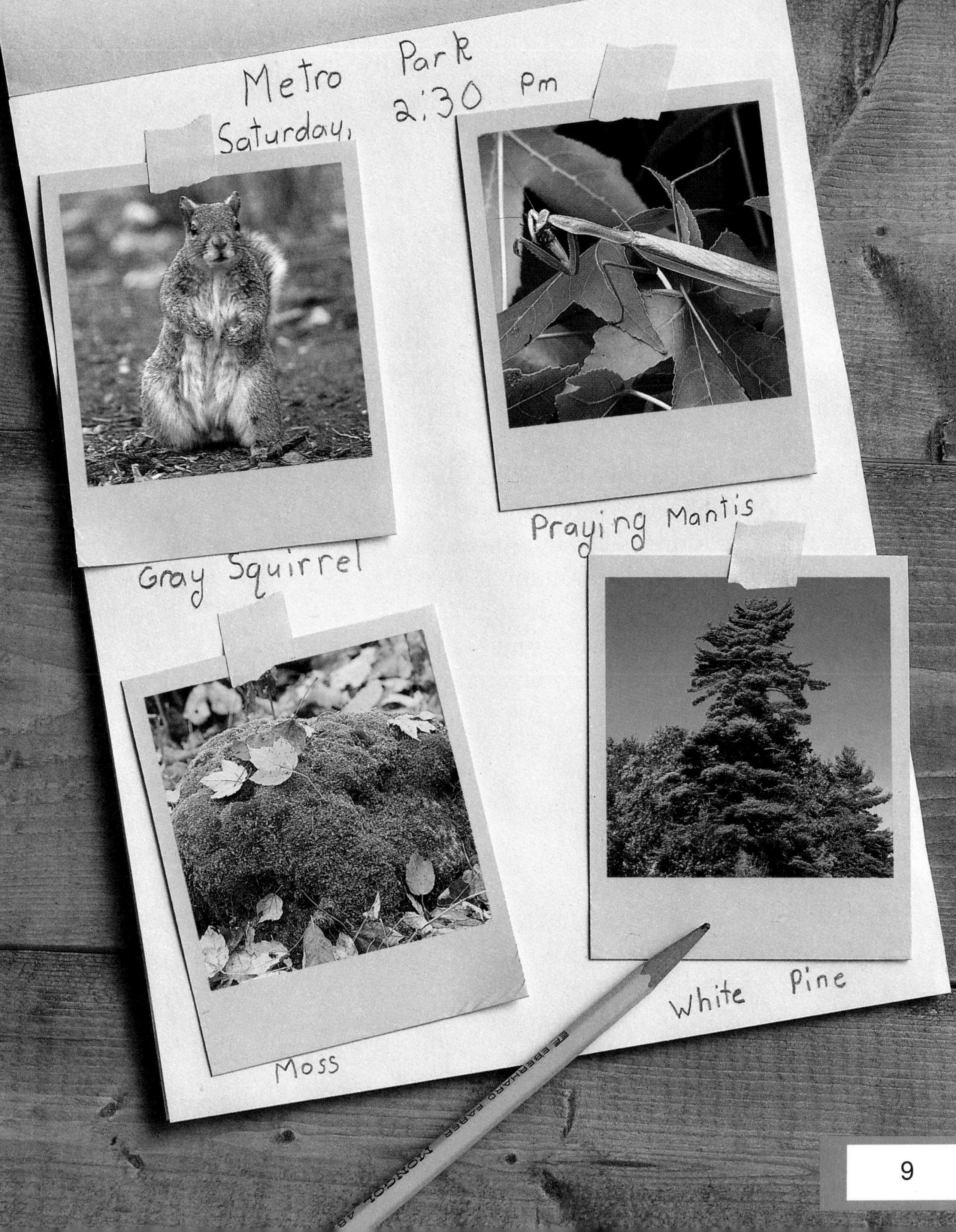

Metro Park
Saturday, 2:30 pm
Gray Squirrel
Praying Mantis
Moss
White Pine
EBERHARD FABER MONGOL 48

Literature 🎭 Link

Science in Literature

Why do plants and animals look and act so differently? Books can help with some answers.

When Hippo Was Hairy and Other Tales From Africa by Nick Greaves.
New York: Barron's, 1988.

Until recently, the African continent had the greatest number of wild animals in the world. This book, with its great pictures, tells you stories about these animals based on African folklore. You'll learn, for example, why the lion does not eat fruit, how the zebra got its stripes, and why the cheeks of the cheetah are stained with tears. At the same time, it gives you facts about lions, leopards, cheetahs, and some animals you probably never heard of. Use this book to find examples of different types of animals and different animal structures as you explore plants and animals.

Other Good Books To Read

Plant Families by Carol Lerner.
New York: Morrow Junior Books, 1989.

Use this book to think about what the parts of plants do and why they come in so many different shapes, colors, and sizes.

The Inside-Out Stomach: An Introduction to Animals Without Backbones by Peter Loewer.
New York: Atheneum, 1990.

Jellyfish, snails, worms, crabs, and ladybugs, as well as some one-celled animals, have no backbone. How do they move? How do they support themselves? Find out their secrets in this book.

10

Insect Metamorphosis: From Egg to Adult by Ron and Nancy Goor.

New York: Macmillan, 1990.

Do you think that all baby animals look exactly like their parents? Before you answer this question, you will want to read the book *Insect Metamorphosis.* In this book you will see that as insects grow, they may look very different at each stage of growth.

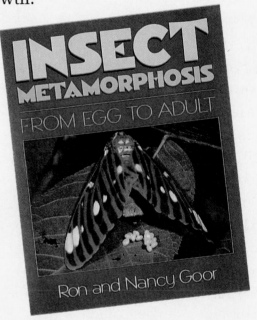

Why the Possum's Tail Is Bare and Other North American Indian Nature Tales by James E. Connolly, ed.

Owings Mills, MD: Stemmer House Publishers, Inc., 1985.

This book is a collection of Native American animal stories that were told to amuse and to teach about nature.

Seeds: Pop, Stick, Glide by Patricia Lauber.

New York: Crown Publishers, Inc., 1981.

This book, with its incredible photographs, tells the amazing story of the variety of ways plants spread their seeds to make new plants.

Mountains. Deserts. Forests. Beaches. Valleys. Plains. Swamplands. Rain forests. Think of all the places to live on Earth. Even if you live in a city, it's probably in one of these environments. Where do you live? Think about the types of plants that share your part of Earth with you. What parts do they have that make them suited to survive in the same place you do?

What's the Point of Plant Parts?

What's the strangest place you've ever seen a plant growing? It sometimes seems as though plants can grow everywhere. You find them in your house, in your yard, and even in the cracks of highways. Some grow in swamps or oceans. Some grow in the dry desert. Some plants thrive under the snow and others live in forests or swamps.

Think about some of the plants you have eaten recently. Do you know how each plant uses its parts to survive? If plants have the same kinds of parts, why do you think the parts of one plant look different from the same parts of another plant?

Scientists do not just guess at or make up explanations for things. They observe something carefully and then use the information to make an educated guess or **hypothesis** (hī poth´ ə sis). Scientists may then choose to test the hypothesis in an experiment. You can hypothesize about plant parts in the next activity.

TRY THIS

Activity!

Why Are Plant Parts Different?

Try observing like a scientist to hypothesize about the different uses of plant parts.

What You Need
three different plants: a succulent, a water, and a flowering plant, such as a cactus, a duckweed, and a geranium; *Activity Log* page 3

Look at the physical properties of the leaves of each plant. What color are they? What size and shape are they? How do they feel? How do they smell? List any other plant parts you see. Observe the physical properties of these parts. Record your observations in your *Activity Log.*

Now use your observations to try to answer these questions. How do the parts of the cactus help it survive in a hot, dry desert? Would the geranium be able to survive in the desert? Could the duckweed survive out of water? Could these plants survive outside where you live? Why or why not?

13

Activity!

Taking Root

In this activity you will observe and measure the roots that grow from four different plant seeds. Begin by asking yourself the following questions:

- What is the purpose of the roots of a plant?
- Why are the lengths of the roots of different plants different?

What You Need

corn, pinto bean, sunflower, and mustard seeds

Activity Log pages 4-5

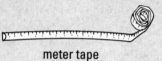

meter tape

masking tape

resealable plastic bag

paper towel

What To Do

1 Place one of each kind of seed in the middle of a moistened paper towel.

2 Wrap up the edges of the paper towel to form a packet. Put the packet into a resealable bag and seal the bag.

3 Put the masking tape on the outside of the bag and write your name on it.

4 Observe your seeds every day for the next seven days. You may need to moisten the paper towel if it becomes dry.

5 Measure the length of each root in millimeters every day and record your data in your *Activity Log.*

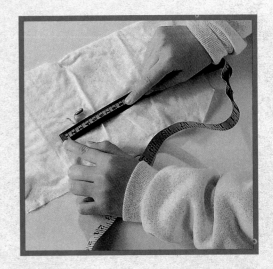

6 At the end of the seven days, prepare a bar graph for each seed using the daily measurements from your *Activity Log.*

What Happened?

1. Did all of your seeds grow roots?

2. Which seed grew the longest root in seven days?

3. Which seed grew the shortest root during your study?

4. Did all the seeds begin growing roots on the same day?

What Now?

1. Use the graph you made to predict how long the roots of the mustard and sunflower seeds might be at the end of ten days.

2. Do the largest seeds have the longest roots?

3. What do roots do to help a plant live?

Looking Ahead

Carefully plant your seeds in a milk carton filled with soil. Over the next few weeks, continue to make observations of the developing plant part.

EXPLORE

Plant Needs

By observing the different types of seeds, you learned that root size and rate of growth are not the same for all plants. But roots perform the same function for all plants and work with other plant parts to maintain the plant. Some plant parts work to help the plant grow. Others help the plant **reproduce** (rē´ prə düs´), or make new plants. Keep this in mind as you examine why the same parts vary in size and shape in different plants.

Minds On! Touch your nose. Do you feel your breath going in and out? Do you feel your skin? Think about how many parts of your body are working together to perform this simple action. What kinds of parts does a plant have to meet its needs? What are some things you think a plant needs to live and grow? Write your answers on page 6 in your *Activity Log.* ●

Plants also get nutrients from other living things. When plants and animals die, they decay and release their nutrients, which return to the soil.

When you look at a plant, you may not see much happening. But even though you don't see it, plants are always busy. Like people and animals, plants have needs. Living things exist on Earth because Earth has certain conditions that allow them to grow and reproduce: light, air, water, and space.

Plants also need **nutrients** (nü´ trē ənts), or certain substances found in soil, to live. Some nutrients come from rocks, which are filled with minerals. Minerals are not living but they contain compounds that plants use as nutrients. These nutrients become part of the soil when rock minerals break up into very small pieces and dissolve.

People and animals learn to stay away from plants that have poison or thorns. The stems, leaves, and roots of poison ivy contain oils that can irritate skin and cause swelling.

Adaptations

Plants that live in different environments have different characteristics that allow them to survive. Over time, adaptations or changes in plant parts have occurred, and they continue to occur to increase the chances that plant species can survive in their environments. Anything that helps an organism survive in its environment is an **adaptation** (ad´ əp tā´ shən). Adaptations are what make the sizes and shapes of plant parts different.

Because they stay in one place, plants must be able to get what they need from their surroundings. Think of all the different types of environments where plants live.

Some plants have adaptations that help them survive.

Plants in the far north grow close to the ground as protection from the wind.

Desert plants grow far apart so that they can get water and nutrients from a larger area. The sharp spines of a cactus keep animals from eating it.

Invent a Plant   Music/Art Link

Try inventing your own kind of plant for the environment in which you live. This will give you a clearer picture of how a plant adapts to its environment. With three other students, discuss what kinds of parts and adaptations you want to give your plant so that it will survive in your environment. Draw a picture of your plant. Discuss the function of each part of your plant. Draw the plant in your *Activity Log* on page 7 and label the parts that help it adapt to your environment.

Activity!

Observing "Breathing" Plants

Tiny openings in the leaves allow plants to take in carbon dioxide and to give off oxygen and water.

What You Need

leaf, hand lens, jar, water, *Activity Log* page 8

Fill the jar with water and submerge the leaf in the water. Observe the leaf for five minutes. Observe the leaf with a hand lens. Record your observations in your ***Activity Log.***

What appears on the leaf? Do you think it came from the water or the leaf? How is what you saw important in photosynthesis and respiration?

Plant Parts

Each part of a plant has certain functions. Leaves, stems, and roots work together as a system to help the plant perform its life functions.

Leaves

Plants don't eat food as you do. They make their own food and provide food for other living things. Most of the food is made inside the leaves.

Roots

*The structures that hold the plant in the ground are called **roots** (rüts). Roots also provide the plant with water and with nutrients that have dissolved in the water. Roots absorb water and nutrients from the soil, and without these the plant could not survive. What types of roots have you seen in your environment?*

Food to Energy

Chlorophyll is used in **photosynthesis** (fō´ tə sin´ thə sis), the process by which green plants make food. In photosynthesis, light energy and certain chemicals are used to change water and carbon dioxide into sugar and oxygen. The roots absorb water and the leaves absorb carbon dioxide. The chlorophyll inside the leaf absorbs light energy. The oxygen is given off into the air through openings in the leaf and the sugar is used as food.

Respiration (res´ pə rā´ shən) is the process by which a plant uses oxygen to change food into the energy it needs for life functions.

*Nearly all plant leaves are green because they contain a chemical called **chlorophyll** (klôr´ ə fil´).*

Stems
*Getting water and nutrients from the roots to the rest of the plant is the job of the **stems** (stemz). Stems also hold plants up so that the leaves can get sunlight. Some stems store nutrients and water for the plant.*

Other Plant Uses

Plant part adaptations matter to you in ways you have probably never thought of. Many of the medicines you take when you are sick come from plant parts. Look around you. Do you see any wooden furniture? It is made from the stems of trees. The paper you are looking at right now comes from the same source.

Because of plant adaptations, we also have a variety of foods to eat. Think of all the different foods you like. How many are plants or plant products? Could animals survive without plant foods?

Plants Around the World   Social Studies Link

Look at the pictures on this page. Decide if the plant is adapted to a cold or a hot environment. Locate places on a globe that each plant might come from. Discuss your conclusions with your classmates.

What are your favorite types of stems, leaves, and roots? You eat more of these than you think.

Rice paddy

Rice

Banana ▲

Banana tree ◀

Spinach ▲
plant

◀ Spinach

▲ Cranberries

Cranberry plant

Sum It Up

Earth has a variety of environments. A particular type of plant cannot live in every environment on Earth. When you move a plant, such as a cactus, away from its natural environment, you may have to make special arrangements for it. It can't survive in a cold, wet place. Plants that live with you would have trouble living in very different environments, too. Their leaves, stems, and roots have adapted to their environment over a long period of time, and any big change could destroy them.

Critical Thinking

1. What plants grow well where you live? How are they adapted to your environment?
2. How can plant adaptations improve the quality of life for people?
3. What could happen to plants if an Earth environment changed from cold to hot?

Flowers for
All Occasions

Like stems, leaves, and roots, the flowers of plants come in all shapes, sizes, and colors. The colors, sizes, and shapes are not just for show. They are important to the survival of the plant.

Minds On! In your *Activity Log* on page 9, draw a picture of your favorite flower. Then, if you can, write its name and label its parts. ●

Activity!

Flower Parts

You can probably name several different flowers. What parts do these flowers have? Why does the plant have flowers?

What You Need

Activity Log pages 10-11

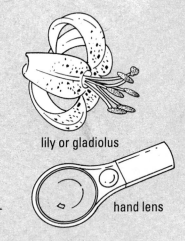

lily or gladiolus

black construction paper

toothpicks

hand lens

What To Do

1 Remove the sepals and petals of the flower.

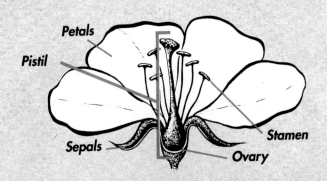

Petals

Pistil

Sepals

Stamen

Ovary

2 Remove a stamen and brush it against the black paper.

3 Use the hand lens to observe the substance that rubbed off the stamen onto the paper.

4 Brush the stamen over the pistil and observe the pistil through the lens. Did any of the substance from the stamen remain on the pistil?

5 Open the ovary with the toothpick and observe it through the lens.

6 Write your observations in your *Activity Log*.

What Happened?

1. Was the pistil sticky?
2. What did you see inside the ovary?
3. What color is the flower?

What Now?

1. Why must the pistil be sticky?
2. What would happen if none of the pollen, the substance that rubbed off the stamen, attached itself to the pistil.
3. Make a hypothesis about why the flower is scented and brightly colored.
4. How are flowers in your environment similar to and different from this flower?
5. Make a hypothesis about the usefulness of the flower to the rest of the plant.

EXPLORE

25

Flowering Plants

In the Explore Activity, you looked at different parts of a flower. Roots, stems, and leaves are all structures designed to help plants survive and grow. The other group of plant parts includes the flowers, seeds, and fruits. Flowering plants use these parts to make new plants.

Seed-bearing plants with flowers have distinctive parts and are called **flowering plants.** Other types of seed-bearing plants have no flowers. Some plants have neither flowers nor seeds.

Parts of a Flower

*The **stamen** (stā´ mən), the male part of the flower, produces a powdery material called **pollen** (pol´ ən). Pollen grains contain male sex cells.*

The flower is the part of the plant in which seeds form.

*The **petals** (pet´ əlz) are the parts of the flower that surround the inside parts of the flower. They are usually brightly colored to attract the insects that pollinate the plant.*

*The **sepals** (sē´ pəlz) are the outer parts of the flower that surround and protect the bud before it opens.*

Wind or insects such as bees are two agents that can move pollen to the pistil.

*The **pistil** (pis' təl), the female part of the flower, contains the ovary.*

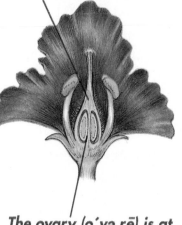

*The ovary (o'və rē) is at the bottom of the pistil. Inside the ovary are female sex cells, which can be fertilized and develop into embryos inside **seeds** (sēdz).*

Pollination (pol' ə nā' shən) takes place when pollen grains are moved from the stamen onto the sticky part of the pistil of a flower.

Once the pollen is on the pistil, a tube begins to grow from each pollen grain. The tubes grow downward through the narrow part of the pistil until they reach the ovary. When male sex cells from the pollen join with female sex cells inside the ovule, which is inside the ovary, fertilization occurs. **Fertilization** (fûr' tə lə zā' shən) is the joining of a female sex cell and a male sex cell from flowers of the same species. The fertilized eggs develop into embryos inside seeds. Both pollination and fertilization must take place to produce seeds that will grow into new plants.

27

Activity!

An Apple a Day

An apple is a "fleshy" fruit because it is juicy and has lots of matter. How do apples grow? Look closely at one to find out.

What You Need
apple, *Activity Log* page 12

Locate the stem of the apple. What is the stem of an apple tree? Look at the other end of the apple. What part of the flower is there? What part of the flower did the apple fruit grow from? What is the purpose of the apple for the apple plant? Draw the stages of the apple's development from flower to fruit in your *Activity Log*. Compare your drawings with those of your classmates.

Minds On! Think of all the ways animals can spread plant seeds to new areas. How can a plant be spread to a new location when a prickly seed pod called a burr sticks to an animal's fur? Write your answers on page 13 in your *Activity Log.* ●

*The **fruit** (früt) is an enlarged ovary. It is the protective covering around the seeds. Do the Try This Activity on this page to take a closer look at the protective covering we call fruit.*

Avocado seed

Apple seeds

Milkweed seeds

Flowers Produce Seeds

All the changes that take place in the flower are designed to produce seeds. Some plants, such as peaches and cherries, produce only one seed in each fruit. Others, such as apples, oranges, and beans, produce many.

Sometimes seeds are planted accidentally, just as flowers are pollinated accidentally. Some plants, such as milkweed, expel their seeds by bursting open and letting the wind distribute them.

Conifers include pines, firs, and spruce trees. They are evergreen and have needle-shaped leaves. Conifers have cones instead of flowers. The cone is the fruit of the conifer. Conifers make seeds inside cones.

Conifer cones

Wild plant seeds are scattered in other ways, too. Have you ever blown the top off a dandelion that has gone to seed? Those tiny hairy parachutes are plant adaptations that help spread seeds. The wind can blow them great distances before they take root and start new plants.

Other Seed Producers

Not all seed-producing plants have flowers. **Conifers** (kon´ ə fərz) are plants that make seeds inside cones. Other types of plants that make seeds without flowers include ginkgos and cycads.

Clusters of fern spores

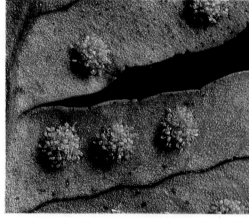

Ferns have stems, leaves, and roots, but no flowers or seeds. The dots on the backs of fern leaves contain spores.

Ginkgo trees have neither flowers nor cones, yet they produce seeds.

Spore Producers

Some plants do not produce seeds. Instead, these plants reproduce by forming tiny cells called spores. A **spore** (spôr) is a cell that develops into a new organism. When spores fall on moist ground, they grow into new plants. Mosses and ferns are common examples of spore-producing plants. Mosses are made of hundreds of separate plants. Each one is a small green structure with tiny green leaves that are only one or two cells thick. These plants grow in clusters close to the ground in wet or moist areas.

29

Variety of Plant Uses

Without plants, you could not survive. Plants not only produce food, they also do a variety of other things. Mosses, for example, hold soil in a forest and prevent it from being washed away by hard rains.

The coal we use as fuel today comes from ferns. The remains of decayed fern plants from about 300 million years ago formed beds of coal underground. People mine the coal and use it as a source of fuel to produce energy.

When we think of fruits and seeds, however, we think of food. What are your favorite fruits and seeds to eat? The next time you bite into a fruit, look for the seeds inside, and think of the fruit as protection for the seeds. Some seeds you can eat. Some people like pumpkin seeds. Some people swallow watermelon seeds. Others throw them away.

Peat, formed from partially decayed moss, is used in many parts of the world in place of coal as a fuel for heating.

Minds On! In your *Activity Log* on page 14, make a list of all the different fruits and seeds you know of that can be eaten. Compare your list with those of your classmates. Make a plan to try a fruit or seed you've never tasted before. ●

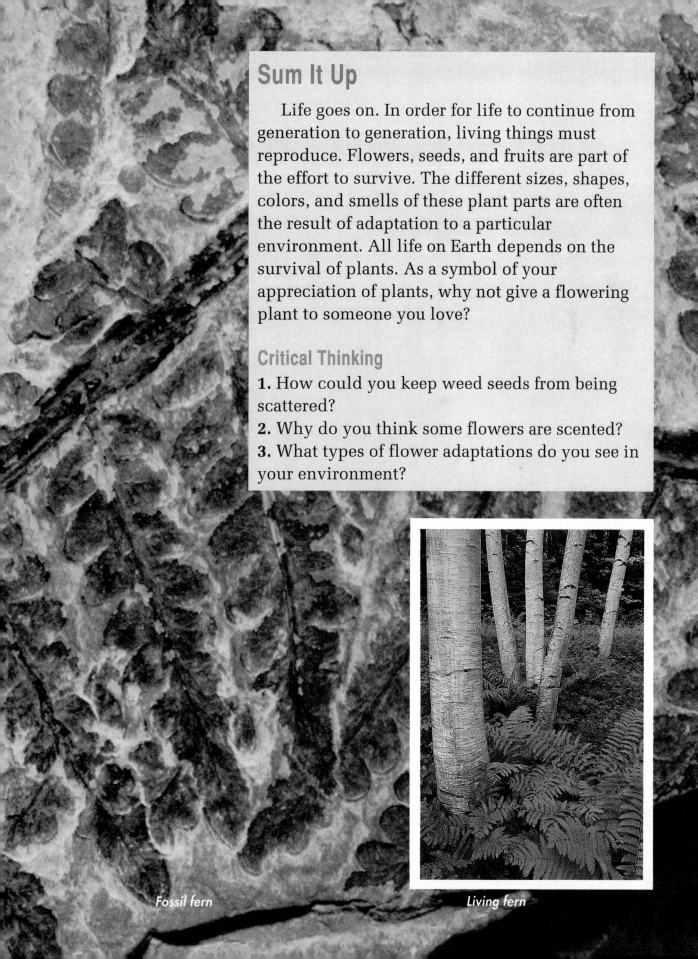

Sum It Up

Life goes on. In order for life to continue from generation to generation, living things must reproduce. Flowers, seeds, and fruits are part of the effort to survive. The different sizes, shapes, colors, and smells of these plant parts are often the result of adaptation to a particular environment. All life on Earth depends on the survival of plants. As a symbol of your appreciation of plants, why not give a flowering plant to someone you love?

Critical Thinking

1. How could you keep weed seeds from being scattered?

2. Why do you think some flowers are scented?

3. What types of flower adaptations do you see in your environment?

Fossil fern

Living fern

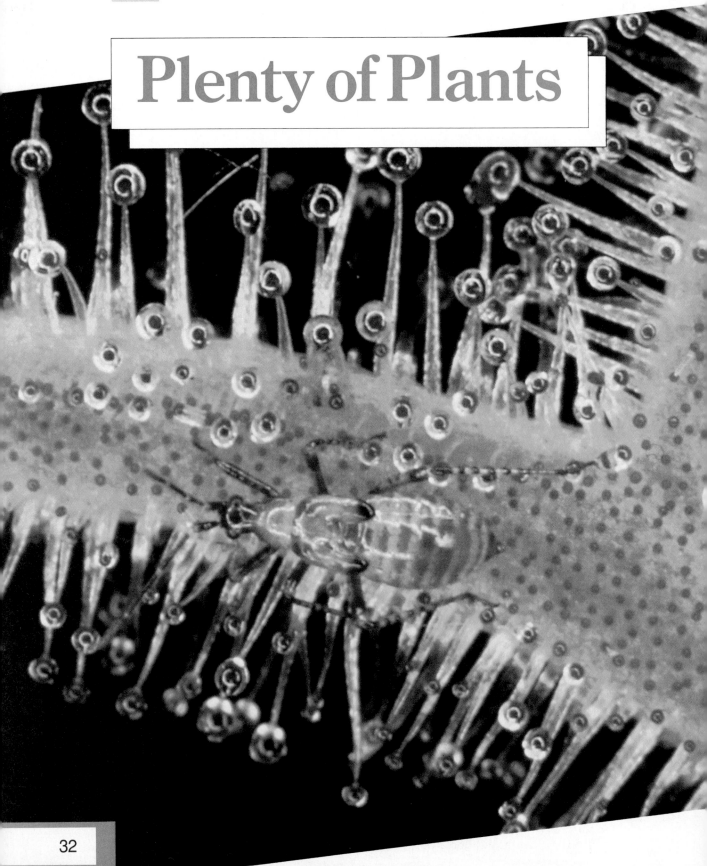

Plenty of Plants

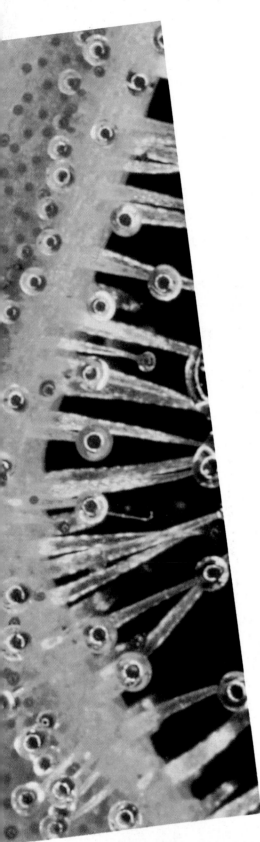

What if you found a plant no one had ever seen before? It could happen. No one really knows how many plants there are on Earth. How would you tell other people about your discovery? How could you compare it to some other plant or animal they already know?

Big plants. Small plants. We eat some of them and build houses with others. Some have flowers. Some are poisonous. There are more than 260,000 different kinds of plants. People are still finding new ones.

People want to make sense out of the world. Even little babies sort or classify food plants they like from ones they don't like. Can you think of other ways people classify things?

What would you say about your plant discovery? You might talk about some of its physical properties—taste, color, size, and shape. What else would you use to classify it?

Minds On! Think about the system you use to organize your things at home and at school. Do you have a collection of baseball cards, rocks, coins, dolls, or stamps? How do you organize your clothes? On page 15 in your **Activity Log,** make a list or draw pictures of the ways you classify your things. Could you use any of these ways to classify your newly discovered plant? Think about how a plant uses its parts to live. That might give you another clue about how to classify it. ●

The sundew plant is able to trap bugs and digest them. However, the mirid bug is able to live on this plant and help eat the trapped bugs without becoming trapped itself.

Activity!

Plant Pipes

You know that plants need water to survive. You also know that the roots are the first to get water from the soil. The roots move water to the stems, which take the materials up to the leaves. But how does the water get from the ground up to the leaves where the plant can use it? In this activity you will experiment with a tube and a flat surface that absorbs liquid to find out which method can move water upward faster.

What You Need

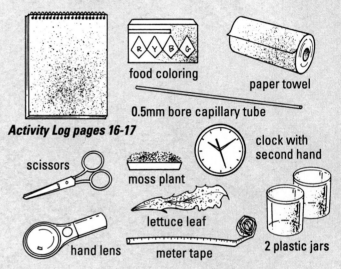

food coloring

paper towel

0.5mm bore capillary tube

Activity Log pages 16-17

scissors

moss plant

clock with second hand

hand lens

lettuce leaf

meter tape

2 plastic jars

What To Do

1 Predict which method will take less time for water to reach its highest level—water rising through a glass tube or water rising through a paper towel. Record your prediction in your *Activity Log.*

2 Prepare a jar with a pencil and a paper towel strip as shown in the diagram in your *Activity Log.* When the jar is ready, remove the paper towel strip from the jar.

Safety!

See the *Safety Tip* in step 5.

3 Add enough colored water to the bottom of the jar to reach a height of 3 mm.

4 Add the same amount of colored water to the second jar.

5 Stand the glass tube into one jar, hold it in place, and time how long it takes for the water to reach its top level. *Safety Tip:* Glass tubes can break, so handle the tube with care.

6 Place the pencil and paper towel into the other jar.

7 Observe and time how long it takes for the water in the paper towel to rise to the same height as the water in the glass tube.

8 Record your observations in your *Activity Log.*

9 Examine the moss and the lettuce with a hand lens. Decide which plant is like the paper towel and which is like the glass tube.

What Happened?

1. How long did it take for water to rise in the glass tube?

2. How long did it take for water to rise in the paper towel?

What Now?

1. How might your results have been different if you had used a wider glass tube?

2. How would a thicker paper towel have affected your results?

3. Which part of your experiment would match those plants, such as lettuce, with tube-like cells? Which part of the experiment would match mosses?

EXPLORE

Getting Water

The Explore Activity showed you how different kinds of plant structures move water and nutrients from one part of a plant to other parts. Some plants, such as lettuce, have tiny tubes that move water and nutrients inside the plant. Other plants, such as mosses, do not have these tubes. Plants that have the tubes can move water and nutrients farther, faster, and easier than plants without tubes.

More than 2,000 years ago, Aristotle (är´ ə stot´ əl), a Greek philosopher, developed a system for classifying living things. He put plants into three groups—trees, shrubs, and herbs.

By the 1700s many new plants had been discovered, and Aristotle's system could no longer describe the differences between plants. Carolus Linnaeus (lə nā´ əs), a Swedish scientist, developed a new grouping system that organized plants based on their structures. Whether or not a plant has tube-like structures like the glass tube in the Explore Activity turned out to be a good way to distinguish between plants.

TRY THIS

Activity!

Plant Veins

What You Need
celery stalk, moss, lettuce leaf, oak or maple leaf, container of water colored with food coloring, *Activity Log* page 18, hand lens

Look at the celery stalk. Find the long strings that run through the length of the stalk. Pull one out and examine it. You are looking at a plant vein. Put the entire celery stalk in the container of colored water and watch what happens.

Next, look at the lettuce leaf and locate the string-like parts. Use a hand lens for a close-up look.

Now, look at the moss. Do you see any tube-like parts? Look at the oak or maple leaf. Do you see any tube-like parts? Why do you think mosses are small and grow so close to the ground? What enables oaks and maples to grow so tall?

If a plant needs water, all you have to do is water the roots. Plants have their own way of moving water from the ground to the stems and leaves where it's needed. How do you think they do this?

To understand how vascular plants work, think about the plumbing in your house. You don't store water in the kitchen or bathroom. Pipes carry the water from beneath the ground, up through the walls of the house, to the rooms where it is needed. In the same way, vascular tubes or veins carry water and nutrients from the soil to the parts of a plant where they are needed.

Plants that move water from the roots to the stems and leaves with tube-like structures are called **vascular** (vas´ kyə lər) **plants.** Vascular plants have tube-like cells that work in the same way as the glass tube in your activity. Vascular plants include flowering plants, other seed-producing plants, and ferns.

Absorbing Water

Plants without tube-like parts to move water are called **nonvascular** (non vas´ kyə lər) **plants.** Nonvascular plants must absorb water through their surfaces in the same way the paper towel did in the Explore Activity. Mosses, algae, and liverworts are nonvascular plants. Because nonvascular plants must absorb water to survive, you will find algae, mosses, and liverworts only in moist areas.

Seeds or Spores

Another way to look at plants is to see how they reproduce. In the last lesson, you looked at flowering plants, conifers, and spore-producing plants such as ferns and mosses.

Why can ferns grow tall, while mosses grow close to the ground?

38

ferns

Ferns and mosses produce spores.

Seed plants include the flowers in a garden, the shrubs around a house, the trees in a park, and the vegetables we eat. Most seed plants protect their seeds inside a covering. Do you remember some of the ways plants cover their seeds? How do plants scatter their seeds?

Plants that reproduce by making seeds include conifers—evergreen plants that make seeds but have no flowers—and flowering plants.

Now think about ferns. Ferns, like mosses, reproduce by producing spores. What category do they fall in if you are classifying by whether plants have vascular or nonvascular structures? Into which category do they fall if you are grouping by how plants reproduce?

Conifers produce seeds.

Why Classify?

Why do you care about classifying plants? Why is it important to know which plants produce seeds and which produce spores? Why is it important to know how plants absorb water? Thinking of the ways we use plants might give you some answers. Next, do the Try This Activity on the following page to form a hypothesis about classifying plants in your environment.

Biosphere Botanist

Would you want to spend two years sealed inside a giant greenhouse? Linda Leigh jumped at the chance. Linda was chosen as one of eight scientists to live and work inside Biosphere II. Linda is a botanist. A botanist is a scientist who studies plants.

Biosphere II is a high-tech, glass-enclosed laboratory built near Tucson, Arizona. This giant artificial environment was built to study how plants and animals grow and interact in five different climates. More than 3,800 plants and animals were put into Biosphere II. Linda was selected to plant, care for, and harvest plants for food.

If you like to work with plants, you might want to consider a career as a botanist. A botanist must have a knowledge of many fields, including chemistry and geography.

Activity!

Plants Outside

What You Need
Activity Log page 19

The next time you go outside, take your **Activity Log** along. Record at least ten different plants you see. Draw a picture of each plant and label it with the plant's name if you know it. Classify each one as a vascular or a nonvascular plant. Then classify each one as a seed- or a spore-producing plant. If you're not sure about a plant, discuss the problem with your classmates. Make a hypothesis. Then figure out a way to test your hypothesis.

Finally, look at your groups. How can you organize your data to show which plants fall in which categories? Compare your results with those of your classmates.

Linda Leigh working on Biosphere II

Sum It Up

The plant parts you looked at in the first two lessons are involved in the life functions by which you classified plants in this lesson. Roots, stems, and leaves all play a major role in vascular plants. These parts work together to give the plant water and nutrients. Flower parts work together to produce seeds. How does a plant system work like other systems? How is it like a highway system? How is it different?

Critical Thinking

1. Are most plants in your environment vascular or nonvascular? Why or why not?

2. Do most plants you know of produce seeds or spores?

3. How are lettuce and ferns alike? How are they different?

Why Are Animals

Animals, like plants, come in many shapes and sizes. And, like plants, animals have certain basic needs that must be met if they are to survive. This lesson examines how animals are adapted to get the things they need from their environment.

Finding a flea on this lion is no easy matter. A flea is so small you can barely see it. You wouldn't have any trouble seeing the giant blue whale. It's as big as five elephants and weighs up to 135 metric tons (about 150 tons). The flea and the whale don't exactly look like cousins, but both are animals. Both need food, water, and air to survive. No matter how large or how small, every animal has what it takes to find food, to protect itself from its enemies, and to survive in its environment.

Built That Way?

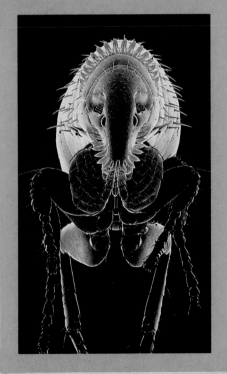

Minds On! If an elephant wants the leaves off a tree, it uses its strong trunk to pull the tree down. How would a monkey get those leaves? How would an insect? What about a giraffe? Write your answers on page 20 in your *Activity Log.* ●

Activity!

Watching Worms

In this activity you will get some idea of what earthworms do deep in the ground and how the different parts of a worm can help it live in its environment.

What You Need

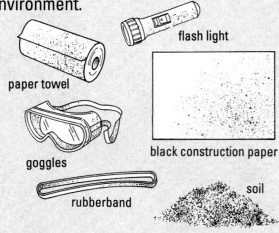

paper towel

flash light

goggles

black construction paper

rubberband

soil

Activity Log pages 21-22

cheesecloth

earthworms

block of wood

plastic jar

small sponge

What To Do

1 Place the block of wood in the middle of the plastic jar. Loosely pack the jar half full with moist soil.

2 Wrap black paper around the outside of the jar.

3 Put the earthworms in the jar and add food. Place the moist sponge on top. Cover the jar with the cloth and fasten with the rubber band.

4 Keep the sponge moist, but do not disturb the earthworms for a week while they get used to their new home.

5 When the week is up, remove the rubber band, cloth, sponge, and black paper. Observe the earthworms. *Safety Tip:* Wear safety goggles when working with rubber bands.

6 Carefully remove the earthworms from the jar and place one earthworm on a moist paper towel. Describe how it moves.

7 Gently touch the earthworm on the head, tail, and middle and describe its reaction in each case in your *Activity Log.*

8 Shine the flashlight on the earthworm. Describe its reaction.

9 Moisten a finger with water and gently rub the earthworm. Describe what you feel.

10 Draw the earthworm in your *Activity Log.* Include as many parts as you can see.

What Happened?

1. How do earthworms move around in the soil?

2. What did you feel as you rubbed the earthworm?

3. What things did you do that caused the earthworms to react?

What Now?

1. What parts of the earthworm did you see that you think help it survive in the soil?

2. Do you think the earthworms reacted differently in the jar than they would have in the ground?

EXPLORE

Body Parts and How They're Used

In the Explore Activity, you saw how earthworms responded to their surroundings and to you. The earthworm moves by stretching its front part and then pulling its back part up.

Different parts of plants are adapted to help the plants get what they need to grow. Animals' body parts and body coverings protect them in their environment.

The grasshopper has powerful back legs and even wings to help it leap and fly.

The sweetlip fish uses slime on its scales to glide through the water.

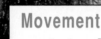

Movement

Animals find food by moving from place to place.

Wildebeests use their strong legs in order to migrate thousands of miles and cross obstacles such as rivers.

46

Teeth

Since different animals eat different things, they don't all have the same kind of teeth.

Animals like the eastern gray squirrel have chisel-like front teeth to cut through the shells of nuts.

The red fox and other animals that eat meat have long sharp teeth for biting and tearing.

Sheep and other animals that eat grass have flat teeth to grind up the grass.

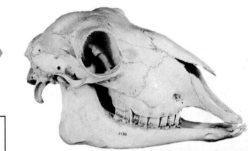

Beaks

Birds have a variety of ways of eating their food. They have different types of beaks to help them eat the foods they need to survive.

Goshawks and other meat-eating birds have sharp, curved beaks to bite and tear their food.

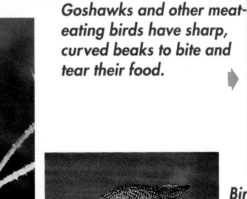

Seed-eating birds, such as the European Goldfinch, have short, cone-shaped beaks to crush and grind seeds.

Birds that wade in the water, such as the marbled godwit, have long beaks to reach beneath the surface to find insects in the shallow water and mud.

47

Eyes

Even an animal's eyes have adapted to help them survive in their environments.

The chameleon can move each of its eyes separately.

The eyes and nostrils of a crocodile stick up above its head, so it can hide under the water and still keep a lookout for prey.

The eastern screech owl has very large eyes, so it can see at night.

Feet/Claws

Characteristics of feet are other adaptations that help animals in their environments.

Mountain goats have hoofed feet, so they can climb rocks.

Gorillas and monkeys have feet that look like hands. They use their feet to climb trees and to pick up food.

Some animals, such as ducks, frogs, and the blue-footed booby, have webbed feet that help them move through water.

Minds On! You have seen some of the ways that body parts help an animal get food, protect itself, and move around. What adaptations do bees, snakes, deer, and skunks have and how do these adaptations help them? Think of other animals and the body parts that help them survive. Write your answers on page 23 in your *Activity Log.* ●

Body Coverings

Hair, scales, spines, and feathers grow from the skin. All of these parts help animals survive in their environments.

Protection

The armadillo lizard of Africa usually runs and hides from enemies, but if it can't escape, the lizard will quickly roll up and grab its tail. If an animal tries to eat it, the lizard's spines make it a hard meal to swallow.

Warmth

Wool and hair keep some animals such as sheep, horses, and pigs warm, and protect them from bites and scratches. The loose, fluffy down feathers that grow close to a bird's body keep it warm and dry. Do the Try This Activity below to get a closer look at how birds use their feathers.

TRY THIS Activity!

Feather Fun!

What You Need

contour and down feathers, hand lens, *Activity Log* page 24

Obtain contour and down feathers of a bird. How are they different in appearance? The thin ribs that branch out from the main shaft are called vanes. Separate some of the vanes, and look at the edges with a hand lens. Draw what you see in your ***Activity Log.*** Next, smooth the feather by pulling outward from the shaft, letting the vanes slide through your fingers. What happened to the separation? Compare the different feather types and how they help birds.

Camouflage

The adaptations that allow an animal to blend into the background of its environment are called camouflage. Zebras have patterns of light and dark colors in their coats to help them blend in with each other. Their camouflage makes it hard for enemies to single out individual zebras.

Mimicry

Some animals are protected because they look like more dangerous ones. This adaptation is called **mimicry** (mim´ i krē). The viceroy and monarch butterflies look alike, but the monarch tastes bad to birds. Because they share body coloring, they increase their odds of not being eaten. Birds learn quickly that butterflies colored orange and black taste bad.

When Hippo Was Hairy   Literature Link

Read Nick Greaves's *When Hippo Was Hairy and Other Tales From Africa.* On page 25 in your *Activity Log,* list five animals you found in the book that have special body parts or body coverings that help them survive. Explain how a body part or body covering is necessary for each animal's survival.

Vanishing From Earth

GLOBAL VIEW

Endangered species are living things threatened with extinction. An animal becomes extinct when every one of its kind has died. Since each plant and animal is a part of the balance of living things, the extinction of one plant or animal can threaten the survival of other living things, including people. The plants and animals on this page are endangered and threatened species.

The North American pitcher plant grows from Canada to Florida in soil that lacks important minerals for the survival of most types of plants. The pitcher plant traps insects inside its long, slender, tube-like leaves and slowly digests them. It is endangered because of habitat destruction.

In the middle 1850s, about 20 million North American bison roamed the western plains. By the late 1880s, only 551 were left. Efforts were made to protect this animal, and today about 15,000 live in wildlife preserves.

The loggerhead turtle lives in the Atlantic Ocean and lays eggs on shores from Europe to the Caribbean Sea. It has become endangered because of beach front development, habitat destruction, and pollution.

Darwin's rheas (rē´ əz) live on the plains of southern Brazil, Uruguay, Paraguay, and Argentina. Habitat destruction may endanger this animal.

Sum It Up

Just because an animal is the biggest and toughest one around doesn't mean it always gets its way. Even small animals have a chance to survive because they are adapted to their environments. How an animal moves and its teeth, eyes, feet and claws, and body coverings all help the animal survive in its environment.

Critical Thinking

1. Can you think of three adaptations you have that help you survive in your environment?
2. Think of an animal that has teeth similar to yours. Are there any other similarities between you and the animal you thought of?
3. Why is it necessary for plants and animals to become adapted to their environments?

The Madagascar (mad´ ə gas´ kər) ring-tailed lemur (lē´ mər) lives in the forests of the southwestern part of Madagascar. Because of deforestation, all species of Madagascar lemurs are endangered.

The wild Asian yak inhabits the cold, dry plateaus of Tibet. It is almost extinct because of overhunting.

Bear cubs learn to climb trees to get away from their enemies, and some chimpanzees use twigs to get termites out of rotten logs so that they have food to eat. How do they know how to do these things?

Have you ever seen a dog do tricks? If so, you know that animals can learn to do things. In Thailand and Malaysia, monkeys are taught to climb trees and pick coconuts on coconut plantations. The monkeys can pick as many as 500 coconuts a day. Botanist E. J. H. Corner used the same kind of monkey to climb trees and break off small branches so that he could study the flowers and leaves. You know that animals have certain parts that help them get food, move from place to place, and escape enemies. Animals also have certain behaviors that help them survive in their environments.

Chimpanzee

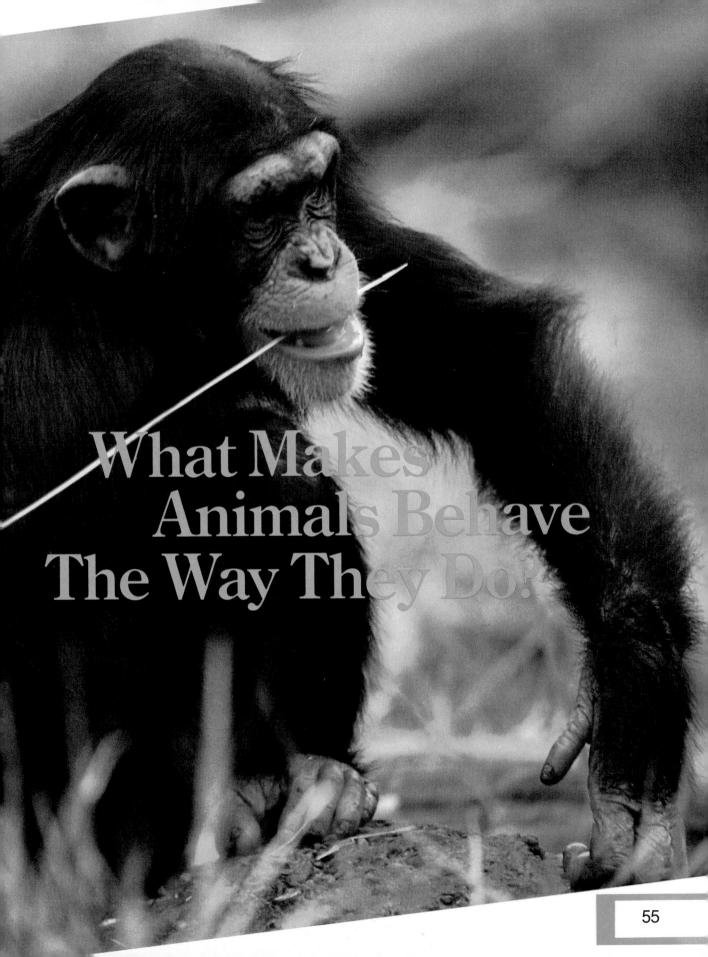

What Makes Animals Behave The Way They Do?

Activity!

How Do Ants Interact With One Another?

What You Need

**Activity Log
pages 26-27**

hand lens

ant farm

What To Do

1 After your teacher has set up the ant farm, don't disturb the ants for a few days.

2 When a few days are up, observe the ant farm with and without a hand lens.

3 Record your observations in your *Activity Log.*

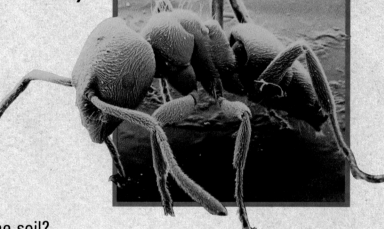

What Happened?

1. How do ants move around in the soil?
2. Are ants strong animals? What have you observed that tells you this?
3. What evidence did you observe that shows you whether ants can or cannot see?
4. Do ants work together? How do you know this?

What Now?

1. What adaptations do ants have for living in sand?
2. Did the ants react differently in their new home than they did in their natural environment?
3. What would have happened if only one ant had been placed in the container?

EXPLORE

Animal Behavior

An adaptation is anything that helps an animal live in its environment. Behaviors are adaptations. Everything an animal does is part of its behavior, or its response to changes in its environment. The ants in the Explore Activity responded to their new environment. You saw the tunnels that they made in their new home. You might also have seen them carry food.

Social Behavior

Some animals live by themselves, while others live in groups. Animals such as fish live in groups called schools to keep each other safe from predators. Animals such as lions live in groups called prides so they can hunt together.

Walruses enjoy sleeping together in one small area.

Prairie dogs dig their holes close together in prairie dog towns. One prairie dog stands guard and sounds an alarm when there is danger.

Behaviors for Protection

Animals' behaviors help them survive. Animals sometimes pretend in order to protect themselves. Pheasants are good pretenders. When an enemy approaches the nest, one of the parents limps away as if its wing were broken. After it lures the enemy away from the young ones, the parent flies away. When a rabbit senses danger, it freezes, hoping the enemy won't see it. If necessary, the rabbit can use its long back legs to run away quickly.

An opossum plays dead until its enemy goes away.

Some animals use other interesting behaviors to protect themselves against enemies. When a vulture is frightened by an enemy, it vomits. The bad smell of the vomit often stops its enemy. Sea cucumbers also use a similar behavior to escape from other animals.

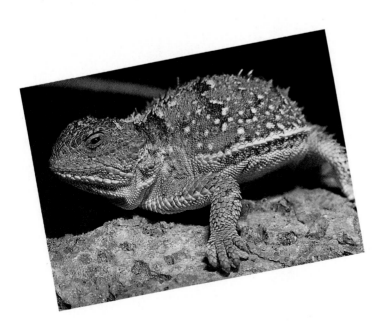

The horned lizard uses a special trick to stay alive. It puffs up with air when enemies are close by so that it will appear too big for some animals to eat. If this doesn't work, it can also squirt blood from slits above its eyes. This may surprise the enemy, and the horned lizard can escape.

Instinct

Instincts are behaviors animals are born with. For example, bees are born knowing how to make honey. A spider knows right away how to spin a web to catch its food. A kitten turns to its mother for milk. A bird knows how to make a nest. Animals know how to find food, mate to produce offspring, and raise their young.

Animals migrate, or move to better conditions, by instinct. Some frogs migrate a few kilometers, while the Arctic tern migrates as much as 35,000 kilometers. Other animals, such as seals, whales, salmon, and deer, migrate in search of food and a safe place to live and raise their young. How do they know where to go? Instinct.

Geese fly together as they move from one area to another in search of food and a warmer climate.

Another instinct that animals have to survive cold weather and lack of food is hibernation. **Hibernation** (hī´ bər nā´ shən) is a deep sleep that helps bats, woodchucks, snakes, and other animals live through the winter. During hibernation the animals need very little energy to survive and can live off the fat they've stored in their bodies. Squirrels and raccoons do not hibernate but they do go into a deep sleep. Instead of sleeping all winter, they wake up to feed. Do the Try This Activity to see how other kinds of animals react when it's dark.

Hibernating bat

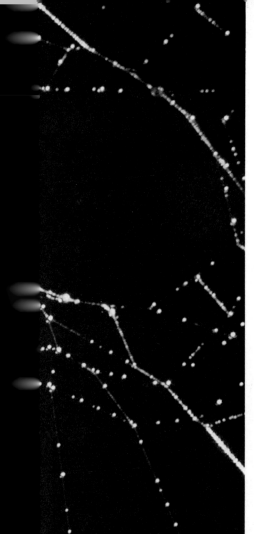

Silk Stronger Than Steel

Did you ever walk into a spider web? You probably think that those thin strands of spider silk are pretty weak. Scientists have learned that, ounce for ounce, spider silk is stronger than steel. That's not surprising when you remember that the spider depends on its web for food. The web has to catch large bugs flying into it at a high rate of speed. The web not only has to be strong, it has to stretch. A spider web can stretch to about ten times its original size. The spider's ability to produce such a strong food trap quickly and without special materials is its own food-getting adaptation.

TRY THIS Activity! *In the Dark*

Do earthworms like light or dark places?

What You Need
paper, index card, 3 or 4 earthworms, *Activity Log* page 28

You will observe the behavior of earthworms when they are placed in a new environment. Place a sheet of paper on a table. Fold the index card to look like a tent and place it on one end of the paper. Put an earthworm on the other end of the paper. Observe the movement of the earthworm for three minutes, then record your observations in your *Activity Log.* Repeat the experiment with two or three other earthworms. How do the earthworms react to their new environment? Can you explain how this is an example of instinct?

Learned Behaviors

You have seen examples of instincts, or behaviors that animals are born knowing. If you have ever tried to train a dog to do tricks, you know that not all behaviors are instincts. **Learned behavior** is behavior that is changed by experience.

A rat can learn to follow a certain path in a maze, a bird called a macaw can learn to talk, and you can learn to do lots of things.

Minds On! How many things have you learned to do? Talk with another student about all the things you have learned to do. These are examples of learned behaviors. How have they helped you? Write your answers on page 29 in your *Activty Log.* ●

Teaching animals certain behaviors can be very helpful. One example of how learned behavior can help us is the training of capuchin monkeys. Capuchins live in the tropical forests of Central and South America. Capuchins are now being trained to help disabled people. They go through a six-month training program where they learn 50 to 100 tasks. The trained capuchins are then given to disabled people to help with tasks such as opening and closing doors and windows, and fetching objects.

Sum It Up

Behaviors are very important for the survival of animals. Some animals live in groups to help them find food, stay warm, and remain safe from enemies. They have a much better chance of surviving in a group than they do if they are alone. Instincts also help animals in their surroundings. A bird knows how to build a nest, what materials to use, and where to build it. A strongly built nest on a high limb will protect the bird and its eggs from enemies.

You also learned the importance of another type of behavior—learned behavior. You have learned to do many things since you were born. These learned behaviors as well as your instincts help you live in your environment.

Critical Thinking

1. Can you think of things you do out of instinct? Can you think of behaviors you have learned?
2. What is similar about working with a group of classmates and living in a family?
3. How is the behavior of animals in a zoo similar to and different from the behavior of animals in the wild?
4. How are both zoo animals and wild animals different from pets?

Capuchin monkeys can be trained to aid people who are disabled.

Reach around and feel the middle of your back. What you feel is your backbone. What animals can you think of that have backbones? Would you be surprised to learn that most animals do not have backbones?

Can you imagine a zoo large enough to hold more than one million animals? That's how many kinds of animals there are in the world. There are lots of ways you could put animals into groups. Big ones. Small ones. Tame animals. Wild animals. Animals that live in the water. Animals that fly. In this lesson you will explore scientific ways of classifying animals.

Plants can be classified as vascular or nonvascular. Animals are also grouped according to the parts they have. But it's not an easy job. Libbie Henrietta Hyman (hī´ mən), a scientist working at the American Museum of Natural History, thought she could compile a record of all the animals without backbones in two big books. After more than 30 years of work and 6 volumes on different kinds of animals without backbones, her work was still unfinished. With so many animals around, can you see how difficult it would be to group all the animals in the world? There are also animals that have just been found and there are probably lots of animals that have not even been discovered yet.

Minds On! Work with a partner to see how many animals you can list in five minutes. On your own, find a way to group the animals on your list. Compare your groups with your partner's. Did you find different ways of arranging the animals? Write your answers on page 30 in your ***Activity Log.*** ●

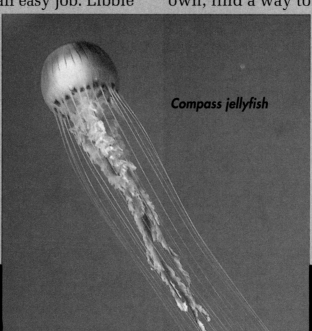

Compass jellyfish

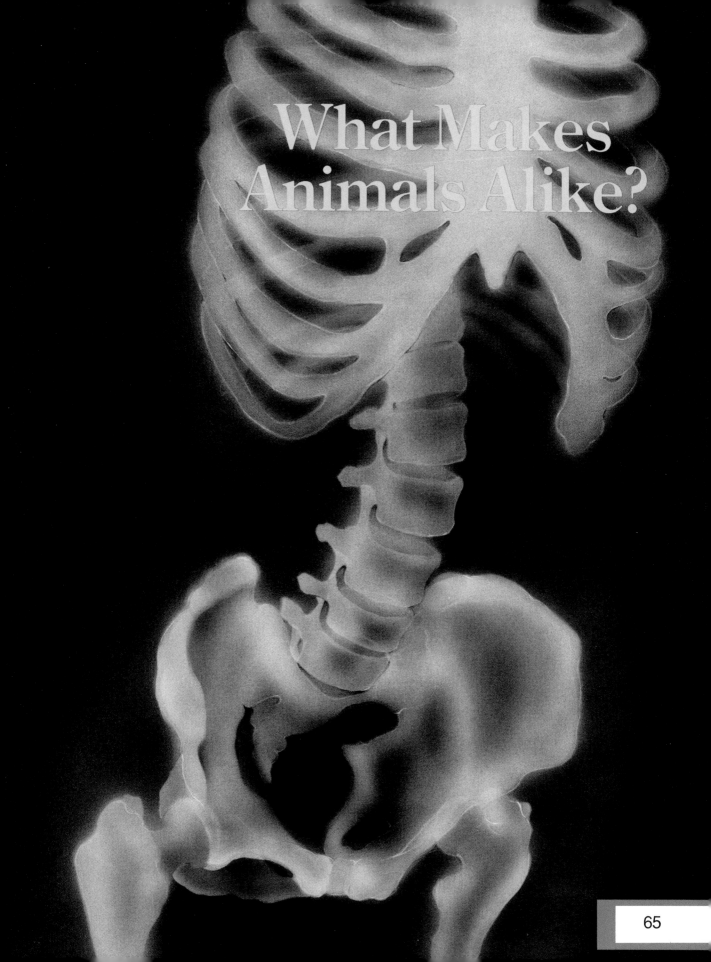

What Makes Animals Alike?

Activity!

Animal Differences

There are many different kinds of animals. In this activity you will observe the characteristics of some animals and use these characteristics to help classify the animals into two groups—animals without backbones and animals with backbones.

What You Need

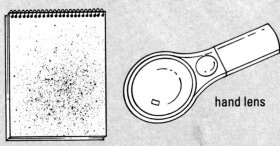

Activity Log pages 31-32

hand lens

What To Do

1 As you observe each of the living animals, answer the following questions on the chart in your **Activity Log.**

a. Where does the animal live—in water, on land, or both?

b. Does the animal have a skeleton?

c. If it has a skeleton, is it on the inside or the outside of the body?

d. Does the animal have a body that is in sections?

e. Does the animal have arms and legs or any other parts that extend from the body?

f. Do you see any eyes, ears, or other sense organs?

g. How does the animal move?

2 Observe each animal with a hand lens. Review and revise any of your answers, and record any other observations in your *Activity Log.*

How does each one of these animals breathe?

What Happened?

1. How many of the animals have a skeleton? Are the skeletons different?

2. How did the animals move?

3. What did the animals do when you touched them?

4. Which of the animals have a body with sections?

What Now?

1. How does each body structure help the animal survive in its environment?

2. Place the animals into two groups—those with backbones and those without backbones. Discuss your answer with others.

EXPLORE

Invertebrates

You have just learned about some different kinds of animals that live in the world around you. Animals have characteristics that make them similar to and different from other animals. Some of the animals had skeletons, sections, legs, or sense organs. You were able to describe how each of the animals moved and to describe its environment. We can use these similarities and differences to put animals into groups.

Snail

*Animals without backbones are called **invertebrates** (in vûr´ tə brits). Many invertebrates, such as worms, have soft bodies. Snails and crayfish are also invertebrates, but they have hard coverings on the outside of their bodies. Each of the animals on these two pages is a different type of invertebrate.*

Flatworms

*The simplest worms are called **flatworms.** They have long flat bodies. Flatworms live in water or inside the bodies of other organisms. A tapeworm attaches itself to the intestine of another animal and absorbs its food.*

Leech

Segmented Worms

*Earthworms and leeches are **segmented** (seg men´ təd) worms. They all have bodies that are divided into rings or segments. They have organ systems for digesting food, getting rid of waste, and moving blood.*

Mollusks

Soft-bodied invertebrates that live on land or in water are called **mollusks** (mol′ əsks). You may have eaten mollusks. Clams, scallops, oysters, and snails are in this group. Many have shells that protect their bodies. Snails have one shell. Clams and oysters have two shells. Some, like the octopus and the squid, have internal shells that you don't see.

Oyster

Crayfish

Arthropods

Insects, spiders, and centipedes are called **arthropods** (är′ thrə podz′). Crabs, crayfish, shrimp, and lobsters are also arthropods. They have an outer skeleton, legs that bend at joints, and a body that is divided into sections. The outer skeleton, or exoskeleton, is shed several times before the arthropod reaches adulthood.

SCIENCE TECHNOLOGY AND Society — Focus on Technology

Great Lakes Zebra Mussels

Zebra mussels look more like clams than zebras. These brown- and black-striped water animals have soft bodies and hard outer shells. They are harmless enough, except when too many of them get together.

Zebra mussels did not always live in the Great Lakes. Evidence indicates that they were brought there on the bottoms of ships from Europe. Zebra mussels were first discovered there in 1986. Billions of them cover the rocks, piers, and boat bottoms in the lakes. They use the food that fish and other lake organisms need to live, and they are changing the biology of the lake. What do you think could control their numbers?

Zebra Mussels

Vertebrates

Because you have a backbone, you have some things in common with other animals that have backbones. Animals with backbones are called **vertebrates** (vûr´ tə brāts´). Their skeletons are on the inside of their bodies, and are made of bone or cartilage. **Cartilage** (kär´ tə lij) is a tough, flexible material that helps support and shape body parts. Vertebrates also have muscles.

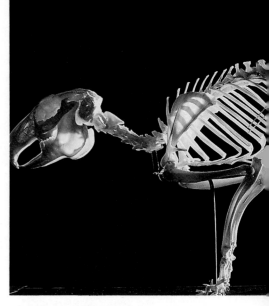

European rabbit skeleton

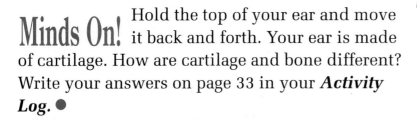 **Minds On!** Hold the top of your ear and move it back and forth. Your ear is made of cartilage. How are cartilage and bone different? Write your answers on page 33 in your *Activity Log.* ●

Warm-blooded Vertebrates

Body temperature is one way to group vertebrates. Of all the vertebrates, only birds and mammals have the ability to control their body temperature. This means that they have the same body temperature when it's cold outside as they do when it's warm. Animals that always have the same body temperature are called warm-blooded animals. Now you know that you are a warm-blooded animal.

Birds

Birds are vertebrates, and most are able to fly. Just as skin and hair protect your body, feathers protect a bird's body and help control its body temperature.

Goshawk chick

Mammals

Mammals include animals such as goats, pigs, squirrels, wolves, whales, bats, and humans. **Mammals** (mam´ əlz) are warm-blooded animals with hair or fur on at least part of their bodies. Female mammals produce milk to feed their young. Some mammals, like whales, dolphins, seals, and manatees, live in the sea. Other mammals are adapted to very warm or very cold climates.

Manatee nursing its young

Mammals produce their young in different ways. Cows, whales, and humans develop in their mother's body and are born when they are completely formed. The spiny anteater and the platypus lay eggs. Other mammals, like kangaroos, opossums, and koalas, are called **marsupials** (mär sü´ pē əlz). When marsupials are born, they can't open their eyes and they have no fur. They crawl into the mother's pouch, where they continue to develop.

Social Studies Link
Mapping Marsupials

Kangaroos and koalas are found mostly in Australia. The opossum is the only marsupial found in North America. Use a map or globe to locate where these mammals are found. Research other animals that live only in certain areas and locate their homes on a map or globe.

Kangaroo with young in pouch   71

Cold-blooded Vertebrates

Some vertebrates are classified as cold-blooded because their body temperature stays about the same as the temperature around them.

Fish are cold-blooded animals. They need oxygen to live just as you do, but they get the oxygen they need from the water. Water flows into a fish's mouth and out past its gills, where the oxygen is collected. Most fish are covered with scales. The scales, like your skin, are used for protection. Do the Try This Activity on the following page to observe a fish getting oxygen.

Bull frog

Giant toad

Amphibians
Frogs, salamanders, and toads are amphibians. The word amphibian *means* "having two lives." An **amphibian** (am fib´ ē ən) *lives part of its life in the water and part on land.*

72

Bamboo viper

Reptiles

Crocodiles, alligators, and lizards are also in the reptile group. **Reptiles** (rep´ tīlz) are cold-blooded animals that have dry, scaly skin. Most reptiles live on land, breathe with lungs, and lay eggs with tough shells. Except for snakes and some lizards, reptiles have two pairs of legs with five toes on each foot.

Hatching crocodile

Activity!

Cold Fish

What You Need
dechlorinated water, jar, thermometer, fish, measuring cup, *Activity Log* page 34

Put two cups of room-temperature water in a jar. Place a fish in the jar and wait a few minutes. Record the temperature in your *Activity Log.* Count the number of times the fish's gills open in one minute. Remove a half cup of water and add a half cup of ice water. Record the temperature and the number of times the gills open in one minute. Return the fish to its home. How does the fish react to colder temperatures? How do you think it would react to warmer temperatures? Write your answers in your *Activity Log.*

What Animals Eat

Scientists who study animals are called **zoologists** (zō ol′ ə jists). Zoologists look for similarities, like backbones, to group animals. Grouping animals helps us organize and understand the system of life. Animals are also grouped by the things they eat. **Carnivores** (kär′ nə vôrz′) eat mostly meat. Sharks, eagles, dogs, seals, and lions are examples of animals that are carnivores. Think back to the types of teeth that different animals have. What type of teeth do carnivores have? Animals like cows and kangaroos feed mainly on plants and are called **herbivores** (hûr′ bə vôrz′). Some animals are omnivores and eat all kinds of food. What are your eating habits? Are you a carnivore, a herbivore, or an omnivore?

Serengeti Plain in Africa

Baboons and opossums are called **omnivores** *(om′ nə vôrz′) because they eat both plants and animals.*

Baboon

74

Sum It Up

You have seen that people classify animals according to similar characteristics. When you listed different animals, you probably thought of more vertebrates than invertebrates. But did you know that 95 percent of all animals do not have a backbone? Examples of invertebrates include sponges, worms, spiders, and all kinds of insects. Since they don't have backbones, they behave and move differently from vertebrates. Vertebrate animals include fish, amphibians, reptiles, birds, and mammals. When a new animal is discovered, zoologists observe the new animal and its environment and then classify it into a group with animals that have similar characteristics.

Critical Thinking

1. If you discovered an animal that had never been seen before, what observations would you make so that you could classify it into its proper group?
2. How are humans classified? Are you an invertebrate or a vertebrate? With which group of animals do you share the most characteristics?
3. If you were a cold-blooded animal, how would you keep your body temperature in a comfortable range throughout the day and night? Throughout the year?

A Lifetime of Change

On the average, you can expect to live about 75 years. Your dog or cat will probably live about 12 years. A mouse will live about 3 years. A horse will live about 20 years. Oak trees can live to be over 200 years old. But no matter how long each plant or animal lives, it changes and develops as it grows older.

Average Life Span of Some Animals

Human	75 years
African Elephants	55 years
Polar Bears	20 years
Horses	20 years
Kangaroos	18 years
Lions	15 years
Squirrels	10 years
Rabbits	10 years
Deer	8 years
Chipmunks	6 years
Opossums	6 years
Mice	3 years

Plants and animals change as they grow. They get bigger. A blue whale grows from 1.8 metric tons (about 2.1 tons) at birth to 135 metric tons (about 150 tons) by the time it reaches adulthood. Plants and animals may also change color. Each major change in an organism's life is called a stage. Every living thing goes through a cycle of different stages as it grows and gets older. When you hear the word **cycle** (sī´ kəl), what do you think of?

Giant Sequoias

Activity!

Fruit Fly Life Cycles

As soon as an animal is born, it starts to change and grow older. You know that you are different from your parents. You have seen puppies grow into dogs. Do you think that all animals go through the same kinds of changes? In this activity you will see an animal change in a way that may seem different to you.

What You Need

Activity Log pages 35-36

fruit flies

banana

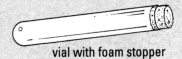
vial with foam stopper

index cards

hole punch

What To Do

1 Place the piece of banana in the jar. Mash the banana with the spoon so that it sticks to the bottom of the jar.

2 Use your hole punch to make two holes close together in the middle of the index card.

Safety!

78

See the *Safety Tip* in step 4.

3 Tap the jar with the fruit flies sharply so that they fall to the bottom.

4 Carefully take the cover off the fruit fly jar. *Safety Tip:* When working with rubberbands, use safety goggles. Put your index card over the opening and put the opening of your jar over the holes. The fruit flies will crawl into your jar in about ten minutes.

5 Wait until there are from six to ten fruit flies in your jar and then quickly flip over your jar. Put the foam plug over the opening so that the fruit flies can't escape.

6 Predict what will happen to the fruit flies over the next two weeks. Write your prediction in your *Activity Log.*

7 Observe the flies daily for two weeks. Record your observations in your *Activity Log.*

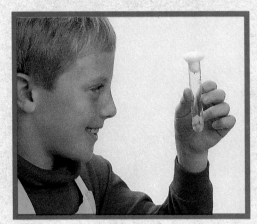

What Happened?

1. When did you first notice a change in the fruit flies?
2. What happened during this stage?
3. What did you observe happen to the animal next?
4. What took place during this stage of the animal's life?
5. What was the appearance of the flies when they emerged?
6. How many days did it take for the original fruit flies to lay eggs and then have those eggs hatch?

What Now?

1. How is the process you observed different from the change a kitten goes through as it grows into an adult cat?
2. Do you know of other animals that go through the same process as the fruit fly as they grow to become adults?

EXPLORE

Life Cycles of Living Things

As you saw in the Explore Activity, the structure of a fruit fly changes as the fly goes through the several stages you observed. Every living thing goes through a cycle of four basic stages: a beginning, a growth period, reproduction, and death. These stages make up what we call the **life cycle** (līf sī´ kəl).

Plant Life Cycles

*Plants, like tomatoes, that grow, reproduce, and die all in one year are called **annuals** (an´ ū əlz).*

1 Germination

*With the right conditions, a root, stem, and leaf start to grow out of a seed. This sprouting of new plant structures is called **germination** (jûr´ mə nā´ shən). Some plants are able to grow from a part of the parent plant. Potatoes, for example, sprout "eyes" that will grow into new plants.*

3 Death

After reproducing, annual and biennial plants die. Although reproduction is often the final stage for a mature plant, that doesn't mean the end of things. The seeds, spores, and new plants that a parent plant produces start the life cycle all over again.

2 *Growth*

The young plant that pops through the ground is called a **seedling** *(sēd´ ling). Without the right amount of light, air, food, and water, a plant cannot mature and reproduce.*

Some plants, such as carrots, are **biennials** *(bī en´ ē əlz), which means that they produce leaves and food one year, and reproduce and die the next year.*

Most trees and shrubs are **perennials** *(pə ren´ ē əlz). They live from one year to the next and continue to grow and reproduce regularly.*

TRY THIS

Activity!

One Potato, Two Potato

What You Need

2 sweet potatoes, plastic jar, water, toothpicks, soil, clear plastic jar, *Activity Log* **page 37**

A sweet potato plant eventually produces flowers and seeds, but there is a faster way to grow sweet potatoes. Here's an activity in which you can see how the life cycle of some seed plants can be changed. Plant a sweet potato in the plastic jar filled with soil and notice where you first observe growth on the plant. Suspend the other sweet potato in the clear plastic jar filled with water and let it soak for a couple of days. Watch to see what happens to the sweet potato. Record your observations in your *Activity Log.* Can a sweet potato grow without seeds?

81

Animal Life Cycles

Animals grow up in very different ways. The life cycle in your activity with the fruit flies was different from that of a plant. It was different from your own life cycle or that of a dog or cat, too. Some animals, such as fruit flies, hatch from eggs. Other animals, like you and the dog or cat, are born alive. Below are the stages animals such as gorillas, humans, and whales go through.

Female rhinoceros and calf

Growth and Development
Childhood and adolescence in humans are the periods of growth and development. As animals get bigger, they learn to survive.

Beginning
Bears, lions, and humans are all born looking like small adults. Even young birds, fish, and reptiles such as snakes, turtles, and alligators hatch out of their eggs looking pretty much like their parents except for their color and size.

Death
Some animals die after reproducing. Others live many years after they lose the ability to reproduce. Both humans and elephants, on the average, live after they lose the ability to reproduce.

Reproduction
Adulthood is a time of reproduction and then aging. Most animals need both a male and a female to reproduce. But, like some plants, some animals, such as flatworms, can reproduce by breaking into two pieces. Each piece will grow into a whole flatworm again.

Metamorphosis

When animals change from one form to a completely different one during their life cycle, as the fruit flies did, that is called **metamorphosis** (met´ ə môr´ fə sis). Butterflies, mosquitoes, wasps, fireflies, ladybugs, and bees go through a complete metamorphosis.

There are four distinct stages in a complete metamorphosis.

Egg

Egg   1
The fertilized egg is laid by the adult female.

Larva   2
The egg hatches into a larva. It's a young animal that looks completely different from the adult. Remember how the fruit fly larva looked different from the adult fruit fly. The larva eats and grows larger.

Pupa

Larva

Pupa   3
The larva stops feeding and enters the pupa stage. It covers itself with a special case. Many changes take place in the pupa.

Adult

Adult   4
After going through the changes, the adult comes out of the pupa. The adult can reproduce to start a new life cycle.

84

Incomplete Metamorphosis

Some animals, like dragonflies, grasshoppers, praying mantises, and cicadas, go through an incomplete metamorphosis. The animal begins as an egg and then hatches into a miniature adult called a **nymph** (nimf). Then it sheds its skin and becomes an adult, and is able to reproduce.

Insect Metamorphosis Literature Link

Read Ron and Nancy Goor's *Insect Metamorphosis.* On page 38 in your **Activity Log,** make a list of insects that go through complete metamorphosis and a list of those that go through incomplete metamorphosis. Put a check mark next to the insects you have seen in your environment. The next time you are outside, look for these insects in the stages of metamorphosis.

A frog has a three-stage metamorphosis. A frog egg hatches into a swimming tadpole with gills and a tail. The tadpole grows front and back legs and its tail disappears. Once fully developed, it moves onto land, and the adult frog breathes with lungs.

1 Eggs

2 Tadpole

3 Adult frog

Why We Care About Life Cycles

Life Cycles of Pests

SCIENCE
TECHNOLOGY
AND Society

Focus
on
Environment

Knowing about life cycles can be helpful in controlling pests, too. Insects, for example, are useful in many ways, but harmful ones can cause problems for farmers.

Biological methods are natural ways of killing insects without using insecticides that are harmful to other organisms. One biological method is to interrupt the insect's ability to reproduce. To do that, scientists study the insect's life cycle.

There are countless ways we use information about the life cycles of plants and animals. Have you ever tasted sweet corn picked at just the right time in its life cycle? There is nothing else like it. Food producers have to know just when to harvest in the life cycle of a plant. If it is too soon, the food may not have the best nutritional value. If it is too late, the food may be too tough to eat. But food is not the only reason to know about life cycles. Scientists also study life cycles to learn how to get along with other living things.

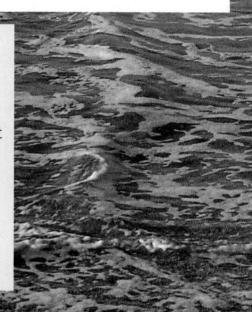

Caring for Young

Did you ever help raise a young animal? Many animals, such as puppies and kittens, depend on their parents for food during the first few weeks of their lives. The parents keep them clean and protect them. Kittens depend upon their parents to teach them to catch mice. A lion teaches its cubs to hunt. Young seals also are taught to hunt. Have you ever watched a pair of birds working hard to find food for their young?

◀ *Male flamingo feeding its young*

Minds On! On page 39 in your *Activity Log,* make a list of rules to help take care of a young animal. You may choose any animal you wish. Think about what it needs to eat and what type of shelter it needs. Then compare your rules with those of your classmates. ●

Sum It Up

Every living thing goes through a cycle. Think about how a butterfly is adapted to its environment as it goes through the stages of metamorphosis. Unlike you, most plants, and many other animals, a butterfly looks very different at each stage of its life cycle.

Living things have a beginning, they grow and change, and then they die. But part of the life cycle of a living thing involves reproducing itself. In this way, an individual may come and go, but the larger cycle of life continues from generation to generation.

Critical Thinking

1. How are plant and animal life cycles the same? How are they different?

2. Why do you think animals and plants often produce more eggs or seeds than are needed to reproduce?

3. What would happen if all the eggs and seeds that animals and plants produced lived?

Some animals are not cared for by their parents. When the small turtles hatch, they must find their own way to the water.

Evolving Plants and Animals

In this unit you've seen that plants and animals are adapted to many different environments. Desert plants and animals look and behave very differently from plants and animals that live near the ocean or in the mountains. The leaves, stems, roots, and reproductive parts of plants can be very different depending on where the plants live. In the same way, animals' eyes, teeth, feet, and body coverings are very different to allow each animal to grow and reproduce in its environment.

Plant and animal adaptations have occurred over thousands and millions of years. These adaptations started as very small changes. An animal may have been changed somehow to let it grow a little taller. This change would have enabled it to reach a few centimeters higher to get food. When survival is the goal, even the smallest advantage is important. In a time when food was scarce, this ability would have given this animal a better chance of surviving than the shorter members of the species. When it reproduced, the characteristic would have been passed on to its offspring. As generation after generation passed, there may have been another change that allowed another one of these offspring to reach even higher. This is how the process of **evolution** (ev´ ə lü´ shən) works. These slow, gradual changes over time give certain organisms a characteristic that lets them survive to reproduce better than others. These organisms produce offspring that are better able to survive. The organisms without the characteristic gradually die off and are replaced by the ones who have it. This process that favors the better adapted organism is **natural selection** (nach´ ər əl si lek´ shən).

Moeritherium (mur´ i thē´ rē əm) lived in and around the swamps and lakes near Egypt about 38 million years ago.

Elephants need large molars to eat the coarse food that grows in their environment. Because their molars need to be so large, their heads need to be large, too. In order to support their large, heavy heads, it has become necessary for elephants to have short necks. With short necks, however, getting food from small bushes and from the ground became a problem. Trunks enabled elephants to get food lower than their necks were capable of stretching.

The evolutionary development of elephants was made possible because their ancestors were animals that could easily evolve in many directions. Through time, the elephant body structure has become specialized because of the environmental conditions they lived with; and now elephants have trunks and tusks to help them survive.

Cuvieronius (kü vē ə ron´ nē əs) lived from the grasslands of the western United States to the Andes Mountains of South America, and was probably hunted to extinction about A.D. 400.

Anancus (ə nan´ kus) lived in the wooded areas of Europe and Asia and became extinct when grasslands replaced the woodlands around 5 million years ago.

Minds On! You've explored many different plant and animal adaptations in this unit. In your *Activity Log* on page 40, write down two plants and two animals. Then describe the adaptations that have allowed them to survive in their environments over time. ●

Sometimes environments change. When this happens plants and animals must move or find ways to get what they need to live and reproduce in the new environment.

Focus on Environment

Growing Deserts

A change in climate can cause farm land to turn into desert. Overgrazing animals, cutting down trees, mining for minerals, or poor farming methods also lead to the formation of deserts. Living on this desert land becomes more difficult. Water and food are much harder to find. Severe shortages of food sometimes occur in these areas. In these cases, the rest of the world may try to help. Should they? What kinds of things should they do? What kinds of things would people living in famine need most?

When plants and animals reproduce, life continues from generation to generation even though individuals die. This is the web of life. You are a part of it just as every other plant and animal you have learned about in this unit is a part of it.

GLOSSARY

Use the pronunciation key below to help you decode, or read, the pronunciations.

adaptation (ad ap tā´shən) a change in a plant or an animal that makes it better suited to survive in its environment

annual (an´ū əl) a plant that grows, reproduces, and dies all in one year

biennial (bī en´ē əl) a plant that grows and produces food one year, and reproduces and dies the next year

camouflage (kam´ə fläzh´) adaptations that allow an animal to blend into its environment

cartilage (kär´tə lij) a tough, flexible material that helps support and shape body parts

chlorophyll (klôr´ə fil´) the green coloring matter of plants that traps energy from the sun and is needed by plants for making food

endangered species (en dān´ jerd spē´shēz) any population of living things that is faced with extinction

evolution (ev´ə lü´shən) the changes in plants and animals over a long time due to adaptation

extinction (ek stingk´shən) the death of every member of a species

fertilization (fûr´tə lə zā´shən) in plants, it's the joining of the female and male sex cells to produce seeds

flatworms (flat´ wûrmz´) simple worms with long, flat bodies

germination (jûr´mə nā´shən) the sprouting stage of a new plant from a seed or a spore

hibernation (hī´ bər nā´shən) a deep sleep that helps some animals get through the winter on little food

hypothesis (hī poth´ə sis) pl. hypotheses (hī poth´ə sēz) an unproved, temporary explanation based on known facts that can be used as a basis for further experimentation or investigation

instinct (in´stingkt´) the knowledge and behavior patterns with which living things are born

metamorphosis (met´ə môr´fə sis) the changing process that some animals go through before they become adults

mimicry (mim´i krē) an adaptation for protection that makes vulnerable animals look like dangerous ones

natural selection (nach´ər əl si lek´ shən) the survival of the best suited or adapted individuals due to being able to reproduce successfully

nonvascular plant (non vas´ kyə lər) a plant that lacks tube-like structures and absorbs water through its surface tissues

nutrients (nü´trē ənts) materials needed by living things for growth

ovary (ō´və rē) the reproductive part of a plant that produces female sex cells

perennial (pə ren´ē əl) a plant that lives from year to year and continues to grow and reproduce

photosynthesis (fō´tə sin´ thə sis) the process by which green plants manufacture carbohydrates from carbon dioxide and water using the energy produced when light is absorbed by chlorophyll

pistil (pis´ təl) the part of the flower that contains egg cells

pollen (pol´ ən) the male plant or spore that produces male sex cells

pollination (pol´ə nā´shən) the transfer of pollen grains to the female reproductive cells in a plant ovary

reproduce (rē´ prə düs´) to produce offspring of the same kind

respiration (res´pə rā´shən) the process by which oxygen reacts with food to release the energy living cells need to function

seed (sēd) the part of a plant containing a plant embryo

segmented worms (seg´ mən təd wûrmz) complex worms with bodies that are divided into rings or segments

sepal (sē pal) the outer part of a flower that surrounds and protects the bud before it opens

spore (spôr) a cell that develops into a new organism

stamen (stā´mən) the part of the flower that produces pollen

vascular plant (vas´ kyə lər) a plant that moves water from its roots to its stems and leaves through tube-like structures

vertebrates (vûr´ tə brāts´) animals with backbones

INDEX

CREDITS